Awards, publication Acknowledgments & American Editions of Love In the Time of Dinosaurs

Awards

• The Isabel & Mary Neff Fellowship for Creative Writing (University of Cincinnati) 1984-1985

• Elliston Prize, First Place (anonymous competition; University of Cincinnati) 1985

• *The Centennial Review* Prize for Poetry (Michael Miller Award) for best poem published in 1984 (Michigan State University) 1985

• Chester H. Jones Foundation Poetry Competition, Honorable Commendation, 1985

• Elliston Prize, Second Place (anonymous competition; University of Cincinnati) 1984

• Elliston Prize, Grand Prize (no other prize awarded) (anonymous competition; University of Cincinnati) 1983

• *Writer's Digest* National Writing Competition, Honorable Mention, 1980

publication Acknowledgments

Portions of *Love in the Time of Dinosaurs* have appeared previously (sometimes in altered form or under different titles, and under the name "Sherri" Szeman) in the following publications:

Journals

• *Borderlands: Texas Poetry Review*

• *The Cape Rock* (Southeast Missouri State University)

- *Carolina Quarterly* (University of North Carolina)
- *Cedar Rock*
- *Centennial Review* (Michigan State University)
- *Cincinnati Poetry Review* (University of Cincinnati)
- *Chester H. Jones Foundation Poetry Competition Winners 1985*
- *Chicago Review* (University of Chicago)
- *Colorado-North Review* (University of Northern Colorado)
- *Cornfield Review* (Ohio State University at Marion)
- *Dark Horse*
- *DeKalb Literary Arts Journal* (DeKalb Community College)
- *Encore: A Quarterly of Verse and Poetic Arts*
- *The Great Lakes Review: A Journal of Midwest Culture* (Central Michigan University)
- *Hawaii Review* (University of Hawaii)
- *Images* (Wright State University)
- *Kansas Quarterly* (Kansas State University)
- *The Kenyon Review* (Kenyon College)
- *Midland Review* (Oklahoma State University)
- *Nebo* (Arkansas Technical University)
- *New Kent Quarterly* (Kent State University)
- *New Letters* (University of Missouri-Kansas City)
- *Ohio Journal* (Ohio State University)
- *Orphic Lute*
- *Piedmont Literary Review*
- *Poetry Today*
- *Portland Review* (Portland State University)
- *Soundings East* (Salem State College)
- *South Carolina Review* (Clemson University)

- *Southern Poetry Review* (University of North Carolina)
- *The Third Eye*
- *Wittenberg Review of Art and Literature* (Wittenberg University)
- *Writers' Forum* (University of Colorado at Colorado Springs)

BOOKS

- *Survivor: One Who Survives* (Ph.D. dissertation, original poetry, University of Cincinnati) 1986

About
Love in the Time of Dinosaurs

(award-winning poems)

Love in the Time of Dinosaurs includes all Szeman's non-Holocaust poetry from 1980-2010. Many of the poems begin with a narrator's or character's questioning his expectations of life versus the reality s/he encounters.

In the section *Portrait of the Poet as a Woman,* the poems, firmly grounded in everyday objects and people, examine marriage, children, and family relationships; eventually expanding the narrator's or character's view to include the universal human condition, especially that of women.

In "Portrait of the Poet as a Woman" and "*A Cappella,*" a new wife feels saddled with and rejected by the young children from her husband's previous marriage(s), despite the fact that she actually loves them and desperately wants their love in return.

In "When Bitterness is all We Have," the long-married narrators rejoice that they have what they consider a more realistic view of marriage than do their children or friends, virtually reveling in how the "bitterness" about life's and marriage's expectations has made them more honest, with each other, at least. Or so they claim.

The narrators of all the family dramatic monologues speak poignantly of our desire for acceptance and love, of the fear of betrayal, of loneliness and isolation even when within a relationship, as well as of treasured moments of love, happiness, and desire.

Imaginative depictions of mythological, literary, and biblical characters' lives frequently appear. In "Cain's Lament," the narrator, Cain, long in exile "in a land that is a good land but far from home" after having murdered his brother Abel, begins his lament against God in bewildered grief but ends in self-confident, righteous defiance, revealing the depth of the character only briefly presented in *Genesis.*

"Ahab's Wife," published almost thirty years before the best-selling novel of the same name, depicts the confusion, longing, and love of a young wife married to an older man whose obsession with hunting the great white whale that maimed his body is so powerful that it continually takes him away from her and their infant son.

The award-winning "Penelope to Ulysses, on their First Night Together after Twenty Years" is a plaintive exploration of how the long-abandoned Penelope, having fought off numerous suitors and preserved her chastity during the two-decades-long absence of her husband, might have actually felt about Ulysses' return, had *The Odyssey* been written from a woman's perspective rather than from a man's.

Some characters who were mentioned in short stories in Szeman's award-winning volume *Naked, with Glasses* appear in poems like "Eddie Madison and the Theory of Evolution," where Eddie simply doesn't understand why his wife, who's returned to school as an adult, keeps comparing him to an ape, and not one from *Planet of the Apes* either.

Eddie's best friend Auggie longs to get closer to God by looking for angels and demons in "Auggie Vernon and the Eclipse," no matter what the personal consequences might be.

In the collection's title poem "Love in the Time of Dinosaurs," the disillusionment, anger, and pathos of Eddie Madison's life as his marriage deteriorates is likened to the changes of the earth and its climate through long geological transformation, leading to an unexpected, startling conclusion.

Szeman's voice is simple and melodic, engaging and lyrical. Her themes are universal, encompassing the perspectives of men and women, adults and children, equally honestly. Though the line-breaks are often syllabic, and the stanzas formal, the language flows musically over the artificially imposed line-breaks. The poems' stories and characters have generated a multitude of fans who claim that, "for the first time, [they] understand contemporary poetry."

All of the poems in the collection have been previously published in literary and university journals, and many of the poems in this collection have been awarded prizes, including the University of Cincinnati's Elliston Prize (anonymous competition; 1983, 1984, 1985), and The Isabel & Mary Neff Fellowship for Creative Writing (1984-85).

Several poems were part of her dissertation, *Survivor: One Who Survives* (University of Cincinnati, 1986). Along with her Holocaust poetry collection, *Where Lightning Strikes,* this collection, *Love in the Time of Dinosaurs,* was unanimously accepted for publication by all outside readers of UKA Press in 2004.

As powerfully written, darkly humorous, surprising, and accessible as her prose works, these poems let you glimpse into the hearts, lives, and minds of ordinary people — whether they be mythological, biblical, literary, or contemporary — as they struggle to make sense of relationships, family, marriage, divorce, children, spirituality, faith, and the existence of God. As they struggle to comprehend the very things each of us experiences every day.

Other Books by
Alexandria Constantinova Szeman

Novels

The Kommandant's Mistress, Revised & Expanded, 20th Anniversary Edition

Only with the Heart, Revised & Expanded, Legally & Medically Updated, 12th Anniversary Edition

No Feet in Heaven

The Kommandant's Mistress (1st Edition: HarperCollins 1993, 5 printings; HarperPerennial 1994, 4 printings; 2nd Edition [with translations of Verdi's opera *La Traviata*]: Arcade 2000, 6 printings), (formerly writing as "Sherri")

Only with the Heart (1st Edition: Arcade 2000, 8 printings), (formerly writing as "Sherri")

Short Stories

Naked, with Glasses

Poetry

Love in the Time of Dinosaurs

Where Lightning Strikes: Poems on the Holocaust

Creative Writing
Non-Fiction

Mastering Point of View: Using POV and Fiction Elements to Create Conflict, Develop Characters, Revise Your Work, & Improve Your Craft, Revised, Updated, & Expanded, 12th Anniversary Edition

Mastering Point of View: How to Control POV to Create Conflict, Depth, & Suspense; (Story Press 2001, 4 printings), (formerly writing as "Sherri")

LOVE IN the TIME of DINOSAURS

(award-winning poems)

Alexandria Constantinova Szeman
(formerly writing as "Sherri")

RWP

RockWay Press, LLC • New Mexico

permissions & publication Acknowledgments

Portions of *Love in the Time of Dinosaurs* have appeared previously (sometimes in altered form or under different titles, and under the name "Sherri" Szeman) in the following publications:

Journals

• *Borderlands: Texas Poetry Review*

• *The Cape Rock* (Southeast Missouri State University)

• *Carolina Quarterly* (University of North Carolina)

• *Cedar Rock*

• *Centennial Review* (Michigan State University)

• *Cincinnati Poetry Review* (University of Cincinnati)

• *Chester H. Jones Foundation Poetry Competition Winners 1985*

• *Chicago Review* (University of Chicago)

• *Colorado-North Review* (University of Northern Colorado)

• *Cornfield Review* (Ohio State University at Marion)

- *Dark Horse*
- *DeKalb Literary Arts Journal* (DeKalb Community College)
- *Encore: A Quarterly of Verse and Poetic Arts*
- *The Great Lakes Review: A Journal of Midwest Culture* (Central Michigan University)
- *Hawaii Review* (University of Hawaii*)*
- *Images* (Wright State University)
- *Kansas Quarterly* (Kansas State University)
- *The Kenyon Review* (Kenyon College)
- *Midland Review* (Oklahoma State University)
- *Nebo* (Arkansas Technical University)
- *New Kent Quarterly* (Kent State University)
- *New Letters* (University of Missouri-Kansas City)
- *Ohio Journal* (Ohio State University)
- *Orphic Lute*
- *Piedmont Literary Review*
- *Poetry Today*
- *Portland Review* (Portland State University)
- *Soundings East* (Salem State College)
- *South Carolina Review* (Clemson University)
- *Southern Poetry Review* (University of North Carolina)
- *The Third Eye*
- *Wittenberg Review of Art and Literature* (Wittenberg University)
- *Writers' Forum* (University of Colorado at Colorado Springs)

BOOKS

- *Survivor: One Who Survives* (Ph.D. dissertation, original poetry, University of Cincinnati) 1986

RockWay Press Trade Paper ISBN 9780977663484
LCCN 2012907384
E-Book ISBN 9780977663422

• Cover Artwork (image "Jurassic Park #12-85") courtesy of Steve Bannos & Gargantua Photos (http://www.gargantuaphotos.com). Used with permission.

• Section divider designed by Francesco Abrignani (collection #12495781), provided by 123RF (http://www.123RF.com) sister company of Inmagine (http://www.inmagine.com). Used with permission.

• Cover design by Alexandria Szeman & RockWay Press, LLC. Copyright © 2012 Alexandria Szeman & RockWay Press, LLC.

• Interior design by RockWay Press, LLC. Copyright © 2013 Alexandria Szeman & RockWay Press, LLC.

• Author Photograph © 2013 by RockWay Press, LLC.

RWP

Visit our Web site at http://www.RockWayPress.com

for
Tom,

Doubt thou the stars are fire,
Doubt that the sun doth move,
Doubt truth to be a liar,
But never doubt I love.

William Shakespeare
Hamlet 2.2.116-119

Acknowledgments

Grateful acknowledgment is made to the people who have read my poetry faithfully over the years, giving me valuable critiques, suggestions, and feedback. I became a better poet because of your unwavering honesty: Becky Keller, Sharon Brown, Terrence Glass, Christopher Williams, Kelly Wingo, Evelyn Schott, and Barbara Walker. Thank you.

To my dissertation advisors, Michael Atkinson, Don Bogen, and Tom LeClair, who gave me free reign to explore my own subject matter, styles, and creative growth while working for three years on *Survivor: One Who Survives.* You represent and encouraged the ideal academic environment, fostering intellectual curiosity, independent thinking, true scholarship, intense research, originality, and creativity.

To former professor, now friend and fellow author, Dr. Gary Pacernick, who began my first college poetry class by saying, "If you ever want to write poetry yourselves and not just study it, you'd better read everything Shakespeare ever wrote and then figure out how to do it better, because he set the standard pretty high." Though I'd already been reading his work since I was 12, you taught me to pay even more attention to the poetry of his language, and to long to imitate its power and beauty.

To renowned author Elie Wiesel, who graciously read the poems I sent him in 1990, though not all in the sample were on the Holocaust, then sent me a handwritten letter of praise. (And when I called his assistant to give him a message of thanks, he didn't chastise me for asking him what he was doing answering his own phone. He simply said, "My assistant isn't in yet: I should just let the phone ring?") You were so kind to discuss the poems with me when I called, and to remind me to keep you informed with what happened with my poetry collections: I was honored beyond belief.

To Andrea Lowne, Publisher of UKA Press [United Kingdom Authors Press], and to its outside readers & judges — all authors, editors, and publishers themselves — who gave me the best critique I could have ever gotten by not only accepting *Love in the Time of Dinosaurs,* but by unanimously accepting it. Blessings to all of you for granting an unknown poet what all poets dream of: an international audience. I am honored to be associated with UKA Press.

I also want to thank Andrea Lowne for allowing me to do the e-book version of *Love in the Time of Dinosaurs* before UKA Press was ready to do the Trade Paper edition. Your professional grace, respect, and courtesy is part of what makes me honored to have my name associated with your Press.

To Spike, Zoë, Vinnie, Hannah, Zeke, and Mosie: thank you for your unconditional love while you were in our lives, as well as for lying on my desk and computer every single day while I wrote. You are in my heart forever.

To Shooter Tov, Mr. Eli, Trixie, Ling, Sascha, Sophie, and Sadie-Doggie: rescuing you increased my own happiness a thousand-fold. Thanks for running into my office ahead of me every single day and keeping me company when I work.

To A, G, and P: with all my love, from the moment each of you was born until the end of time. But you know that.

To Tom, who likes to brag that my "poetry is the only good poetry" he's ever read, and that it's "lots better than 'The Midnight Ride of Paul Revere' by Longfellow," which he can still quote verbatim: you're the love of my life, and not just because you like my poetry.

Table of contents

Author Bio, Photo, Amazon Page, Web-site, Twitter, Blog, & Contact Information

Love in the Time of Dinosaurs

Love In the Time Of Dinosaurs

As we grow up,
we become strangers
to ourselves.

Sigmund Freud

Cain's Lament

Yes, this is the landscape I heard of once,
but it told me things I didn't believe in.

I was so young then: I didn't know this
wandering. It's been a long, hard time, this

waiting for rain in a land that drinks sweat,
then blasts men's eyes with sand. A long, hard time,

grinding my past into the heart of each
stranger, not knowing why You didn't stay

my hand. It's enough, this dry earth crumbling,
this debt owed and never paid. I'm tired of

hearing my children cry when there's nothing
to eat, tired of taking my wife in the

dark or from behind because I can't bear
her eyes on me when the light glares too cold,

tired of seeking a city that's a good
city but far from my home. All these long

years, never to start anew, when one hour
with those who loved him would have been more than

punishment enough. All these years never
to forget, never to be forgiven.

It's too much to pay for Your indifference,
too much for wondering why You more

than I, when I, too, bring forth life from the
earth, when I forgive those who have wronged me,

when I humbly take into my house those
who have sinned, those who have suffered enough.
ॐ

Field Trip to the Serpent Mound

Once again our professor reminds us that we
have not come here to see the Serpent Mound but to see the

geological formations beside it, and
because we want the ten weeks' credit for only

five long, hot summer days, we dutifully turn our
attention back to the area, nearly five

miles in diameter, containing extremely
faulted and folded bedrock, Paleozoic

carbonates, sandstones, and shales, dutifully noting shatter
cones and the vertical fractures in the rock, all

uncommon in the normally flat-layered rocks
of Ohio, even southwest Ohio. But

it's the Serpent Mound that draws our eyes again and
again. That nearly quarter-mile embankment of

earth built by Indians a thousand years ago,
the gigantic snake uncoiling in seven deep

curves along a bluff overlooking Brush Creek, the
oval embankment near the end of the bluff most

probably representing the open mouth of
the serpent as it strikes. It's the largest and finest

snake effigy mound in North America and was
not built over any burials or remnants

of living areas as everyone once thought,
its massive body uncoiling, its huge earthen

mouth unhinged and open, ready to swallow down
anything foolish or blind enough to stumble

into its path. With an exasperated sigh,
the professor reminds us how the landowners

have been most cooperative in allowing us
to examine the site and will we please respect

their property and disturb it as little as
possible and please pick up that empty plastic

bag lying there in the thick ground vegetation
and will we shirkers please pay attention for once

in our lives? We obediently huddle around him, scribbling all
his words in our spiral-bound notebooks, thinking of

Moses instead, casting his rod down before the
Pharaoh so it might turn into a serpent and

devour all the serpents conjured up by the
Pharaoh's magicians and sorcerers. In a drone,

the professor points out the exposed bedrock and
the dolomite, shattered and brecciated, but we

think about snakes digesting everything but hair
and feathers, even teeth and bones. We think about

curved fangs and glistening scales and the tremendous size
of it all. During lunch with his favorite students,

Love in the Time of Dinosaurs

gulping down tuna salad on toasted rye, the
professor explains that researchers have been studying the

possibility that the effigy may have
been laid out in alignment with various and

sundry astronomical observations. The
professor discusses the closely spaced fractures

and the undisturbed Pleistocene glacial till, while
we shirkers tiptoe around the Serpent Mound,

whispering about Medusa, her voluptuous
body and writhing nest of serpent-hair turning

us hard as stone. About the sweet illicit taste
of forbidden fruit and afterward our crawling

on our bellies and eating dirt all the days of
our lives, gladly, so gladly, with the sweet taste of

the fruit forever on our lips and tongue. After
lunch the professor patiently explains why the

Serpent Mound disturbance cannot be explained by
either the meteorite- or comet-impact hypotheses

or by the gas-explosion theory but may be
somewhat if only incompletely understood

as the result of some ancient volcanic or
tectonic activity, but we're thinking of

Cleopatra, with her dark hair and her milky
white breasts, bared to fangs which, when not in use, fold back

and lie flat, but which when used, spring forward and then
become erect. Serpent bodies long and cool and

hard, muscles undulating beneath taut snake skin.
Vipers' pits seeking out the heat, the damp moist heat,

trembling to the vibrations which reach us through the
faulted and folded Paleozoic structures.

Which stir us from our underground dens and thrust us
violently up along the fault lines, our bedrock

exposed. Which leave us shattered, gasping and spent, our
snake hearts dark and deep as the earth from which we came.
ଔ

Eddie Madison and the Theory of Evolution

There is something basically, inherently, and
undeniably wrong about any theory

that says that man — the most beautiful and noble
of any of God's creatures — that man, who has walked

on the moon's surface, harnessed electricity,
and invented the polio vaccine — that man,

who walks upright sometimes as early as nine months
and who can speak all kinds of languages, even

Pig-Latin — that this glorious creation of
God's could possibly be descended from apes. At

least, that's how it seems to Eddie Madison of
Scranton, Pennsylvania, and he should know since he's

a real man and he's looked it up in the Bible
besides. He tries to explain the inherent and

inescapable wrongness of such a theory
to his wife every time she comes home from the night

class she's taking at the local community
college, but she throws words back at him, unpleasant

words like *reptilian brain* and *amphibious
mammalian* something-or-other, real ugly words

that Eddie Madison's willing to bet at least
$50 are aimed directly at him, no

matter how many times his wife tries to deny
it. Eddie Madison just doesn't understand

what she's so mad about these days. After all, it's
not his fault that God made man first and only made

woman later almost as an afterthought and
out of a rib-bone besides. It's not his

fault that Eve disobeyed and ate a piece of that
forbidden apple and is therefore condemned to

a lower place in the world's scheme of things and to
suffer the pangs and agonies of childbirth while

man suffers only the sweat of his brow and the
toil of his labor, the pains of which a few beers

after work can easily dissipate. After
all, Eddie Madison didn't make up the rules —

he just has to live by them. Of course, when Eddie
said that to his wife last Tuesday night when she got

home after class, she grabbed her own hair with both fists
and made these terrible, horrifying, screaming,

choking noises, then threw the dinner casserole
right at the wall next to his head, while the dish was

still full of hamburger-macaroni. Eddie
was most sincerely upset and unpleasantly

surprised by this entire flying-casserole-
dish episode, and not just because his wife went

to sleep in the spare bedroom and still hasn't cleaned
all the hamburger-macaroni off the wall.

And Eddie Madison is most certainly not
upset because his wife has slept in the spare room

every single night since then, though sometimes he does
get incredibly, achingly lonely in that

king-sized bed and spend most of the night staring at
the infinite and unfathomable darkness

of the ceiling, which seems to him symbolic of
something bigger and greater than he himself is,

if only he knew how to understand it all.
No, what Eddie Madison's upset about is

this unnatural origin-of-species thing,
this ape-into-man theory that's got his docile,

sweet-tempered wife staying out Tuesday and Thursday
nights after class and throwing still-full casserole

dishes at him. Not that an empty dish would have
been any better, mind you, but it would have been

somehow less offensive, less emasculating.
And now that Eddie Madison's on the topic,

he's not too crazy about the word *descent* in
this ape-to-man survival-of-the-fittest thing

either, with its rather nasty implication
that some mangy, knuckle-dragging chimp named Cheetah

could be higher on the evolutionary
scale than Eddie Madison of Scranton, PA.

And now that he's finally figured out exactly
what's bothering him, Eddie's going to tell his

wife. Just as soon as that short-haired bull-dyke classmate
of hers who always gives her a ride now that she's

not allowed to use the station-wagon any
more brings her home tonight, Eddie's going to tell her

exactly and explicitly what he thinks of
Darwin's whole ape-to-man natural-selection

descent thing, and for once she's going to listen
to him. That's why he's sitting there, in the living

room, in the dark, with the open Bible by his
left hand and the loaded revolver by his right,

so he can explain to his wife once and for all
how God's absolutely perfect perfection and

infinitely wise wisdom meticulously
and purposely placed woman beside man — slightly

lower, it's true — but beside man nevertheless.
Under his arm for protection and near his heart

for love. And Eddie Madison does love his wife.
He never meant to hit her like that. He'll tell her

that, too. Right after he's demolished the theory
that's so disrupted and disturbed his life. And she'll

be grateful to him for explaining it all so
clearly. Then Eddie Madison will be able

to sleep at night, secure in the knowledge that he
has returned the universe to its intended

order. That he, Eddie Madison, has restored
man to his rightful place in God's great scheme of things.

That he, Eddie Madison of Scranton, PA,
is not descended from the lowly and bestial

apes as some would have him believe, but is, instead,
more celestial than the angels themselves before

they fell, their glorious wings aflame, into the
black and bottomless pit that waits beneath us all.
ଔ

Alexandria Constantinova Szeman

Auggie Vernon and the Eclipse

He has everything he needs set up in the back
yard: two triangular UPS shipping tubes
held together by duct tape in the middle, with
a pin-pricked piece of foil on one end and a piece
of white paper on the other end of the box,

inside, near the viewing portal. Several pairs of
dark Ray-Ban sunglasses, each pair larger than the
last so Auggie can wear more than one pair at the
same time. A welder's glass. The Bible. And cousin
Vern's brand new, high-powered telescope, which

Auggie had to sneak into the basement while his
wife was at work because she's a nurse and has been
scaring everyone with her warnings about light-
induced retinal injuries, which can occur
without any discomfort or pain since there are

no pain-receptors in the retina and which
don't occur for at least several hours after
the damage is done. But nothing's going to stop
Auggie from seeing the full solar eclipse, though
he's not interested in the eclipse itself. No,

he's not interested in the color of the sky
changed by the refraction of light. He doesn't
care if birds or bats or other animals get
confused and prepare themselves for night. He 's simply
not concerned with the umbra, that vast shadow

14

of totality rapidly advancing like
a tidal wave across the landscape towards him. And
he doesn't care about the photosphere shining
through lunar valleys and creating Baily's Beads
— a familiar feature of total eclipses —

when the razor-thin solar crescent breaks into
a chain of bright beads as the moon covers the sun.
Or the Diamond Ring effect, when the sun's inner
corona forms a wedding band around the moon
with a single diamond of blinding white light. Or

the solar corona which appears when the sun
is completely covered by the moon, though that's the
only time the corona is visible to
the naked eye, and though the corona looks like
white streamers radiating outward. Auggie's not

interested in the sun's prominences either,
those gigantic, crimson, flame-like jets and loops of
gas around the edge of the sun. No, what Auggie
Vernon's interested in is Hell. And though he can't
find any biblical corroboration for

it, he's pretty sure there's only one place in the
whole universe that's big enough and hot enough
and infernal enough to serve as Hell, and that
place is right in the middle of the sun. So that's
what all these preparations are for — Hell. If he

times it correctly and aims the telescope right in
the center of it all, Auggie figures he'll be
able to see all those damned souls, crammed so close and
tight together they look like urban tenement
dwellers, all of them squirming and shrieking like they're

in a blast furnace, only with their skin growing
right back on the bones after it's melted off so
they can suffer all over again, for the rest
of eternity. And Auggie thinks there's a good
chance he'll get to see plenty of demons, too. They

should be easy to distinguish from the rest of
the damned on account of the horns growing out of
their heads, the leathery wings on their backs, and their
cloven-hoofed feet. And then, if he's really lucky
and his courage holds out, Auggie thinks he might get

a chance to see the Big Guy himself — the biggest,
baddest guy of them all — Satan. Lucifer. Prince of
Darkness. Beelzebub. Mephistopheles. Of
course, Auggie doesn't know what the Big Guy looks like,
but he guesses he'll recognize Satan when he

sees him. Only Auggie won't have to shout, *Get thee
behind me,* 'cause he'll be safe here on earth, about
a billion-trillion light-years away from the sun.
And according to Auggie's calculations, the
best time to see Hell is right after the solar

eclipse, when the Devil thinks he's still hidden by
the moon. After Auggie's seen Hell and can describe
the Devil to everyone else, he won't have to
worry that his unemployment benefits ran
out or that his wife is threatening to divorce

him unless he finds another job. Why, people
from all over the world will just throw money at
him — piles and piles of money — just for the privilege
of hearing Auggie Vernon talk about Hell. Oh,
yes, Auggie thinks as he puts down the taped shipping

tubes and takes off the welder's glass, it'll be worth
retinal damage, with or without pain. Oh, yes, he
thinks, as he aims the telescope toward the sun, it
would even be worth eclipse-blindness, despite the
fact that his cousin Vern tried to scare him, saying

that Satan's face, as the last thing Auggie saw, would
be burned on Auggie's retina and would be the
only thing he'd see for the rest of his life. Vern
was jealous 'cause he hadn't thought of looking for
Hell himself. Yes, Auggie thinks, as he pulls off the

sunglasses, if only he's brave enough to look
at the Devil's face, he'll be a bigger man than
anyone else in the history of the whole
human race. If he can look the Devil in the
eye without flinching, he'll learn all the secrets

of the universe. Except for the ones that God
didn't even tell the angels before they fell.
It'll be the closest Auggie Vernon ever
gets to fame and immortality, he thinks as
he takes a deep breath, grabs his Bible, and raises

the telescope to the fierce light of the sun. It's
the closest Auggie Vernon will ever get to
being somebody important, the closest he'll
ever get to respect, the closest he'll ever get to
beholding the ever-radiant face of God.

CB

Alexandria Constantinova Szeman

Love in the Time of Dinosaurs

Many suggestions have been put forward
in favor of a dramatic end to the dinosaurs:
through flips in the [earth's] magnetic field,
exploding stars, or comet or meteorite impacts.
Most have been dismissed…because they…
represent simplistic attempts
to link the big and dramatic dinosaurs
with an equally big and dramatic ending.

David Norman
Dinosaur

There is something disturbing, unsettling, and most
extremely frightening about having your wife keep

insisting that you're living in the Ice Age, and
Eddie Madison doesn't understand it at

all. Though he does have to admit that lately it's
been pretty frosty around the house, especially

since his wife got really mad, threw a hot dish of
hamburger-macaroni at him and started

sleeping in the spare bedroom. And Eddie doesn't
understand why she keeps complaining about Charles

Darwin and apes taking over the world. Charlton
Heston was the star of *Planet of the Apes*. In

18

fact, Eddie doesn't remember a Charles Darwin
in any of the *Planet of the Apes* movies,

unless he was one of those ape extras and he
didn't even get his name in the credits. And

Eddie most certainly doesn't understand why
his wife keeps calling him a dinosaur, in a

tone of voice that makes it sound like an insult, and
not just any dinosaur, but a stupid one

like *Brachiosaurus*, whose head looks about the
size of a fist in comparison with the rest

of its body. Eddie wouldn't have minded if
she'd called him a *Tyrannosaurus Rex* or a

Velociraptor. He's seen *Jurassic Park* three
times, so he knows what T. Rex and those bad Raptors

can do to people and cars and even buildings.
But a *Brachiosaurus*? As far as Eddie

Madison is concerned, a *Brachiosaurus*
doesn't even sound like a dinosaur. It sounds

more like a disease you'd get from smoking or from
cleaning asbestos out of walls. And Eddie just

doesn't understand why his wife stopped making the
kids' clothes and keeping up the house and canning the

garden vegetables. Since she started taking those
community college classes, all she has time

for is Darwin, Freud, and Marx. Eddie Madison
doesn't believe in Darwin or Freud or Marx. But

now instead of having basement shelves filled with canned
spaghetti sauce and pickles and onion relish,

instead of having a hot dinner waiting for
him when he gets home from work, Eddie's got a wife

who's throwing hamburger-macaroni at him,
sleeping in the extra bedroom, and complaining

about glaciers and icebergs
and bone-chilling winds.

Fossil Evidence

But at night, when Eddie sifts through the landscape of
their lives together, he remembers his wife — in

bed, her belly big and round with their first child, her
huge belly glowing white in the faint moonlight. He

remembers his hands moving reverently over
the stretched skin, his head lowering till his ear lay

against her, his own heart pounding at the sound of
their unborn child. Eddie digs deeper and recalls

standing over the cradle as the baby sleeps,
her mouth open and smelling of milk, his fingers

brushing her skin, then coming away with the faint
scent of baby powder on them. As he brushes

away the dust and debris of the last few years
he finds the memory of his wife shaking out

the laundry, damp piece by damp piece, then draping it
over the line, the sunlight casting her shadow

on the ground, the wind snapping and fluttering the
clean white sheets while, on the other side of the yard,

Eddie lifted his daughter, holding her by one
arm and one leg, then swinging her around, his hands

strong and secure, his solid legs planted like trees
to support her slight and insubstantial weight, her

shrieks and giggles splitting the early morning air.
He lifts the heavy rocks and remembers the night

he stood in the open doorway, waiting for his
wife as she waded slowly across the rain-soaked,

muddy yard, her legs wide, her hand pressed into the
small of her back, her huge belly hanging so low,

it seemed it would touch the ground. And he remembers
the trail of footsteps she left behind her, still there

the next spring when the snow finally melted, the trail
hardened and rocky in the vast and empty yard.

Continental Drift

When the ground first fractured beneath him, Eddie was
waking up alone in the middle of the night,

finding his wife, at last, in the kitchen, with her
dark head resting on one of her open textbooks,

balls of crumpled paper on the floor around her
feet, the sun blinding him as it sparked around the

edges of the window blinds. The heat welled up through
the faults in his life's surface, and after a long

day at the body plant, he came home to find the
house dark, the stove cold, his girls, whining and sleepy,

waiting impatiently for him on the front porch,
holding a note from his wife which said simply, *Feed*

them and put them to bed. There were collisions and
earthquakes, fierce heat, and bitter unforgiving cold.

Eddie felt like he and his two girls were on one
continent with his wife on another, drifting

further and further away from them, until an
entire ocean was flooding the space between

them. And he remembers most bitterly sitting
at his father's coffin, gripping his mother's hand,

his eyes so swollen they were beyond weeping, his
daughters sitting stiffly on the cold metal chairs

in the row behind him, creasing and flattening
the pleats of their crisp, new dresses, smiling bravely

at Eddie every time he turned around to look
at them. When the ground he and his girls were standing

on separated at last from the earth around
it, his wife was a hundred-thousand miles away.

Ice Age

There may, indeed, have been extended periods
when the earth's continents were securely joined, when

there were no polar ice caps, when great dinosaurs
roamed the earth as its undisputed masters, when

Love In the Time Of Dinosaurs

Eddie and his wife were actually happy. It's
a fact that the growth and retreat of glaciers in

response to changes in the global climate can
cause the extinction of entire species. And

marriages. Eddie Madison learned all of this
without his ever having gone to college. And

somehow, without ever being told, Eddie knows
that even if this crushing glacier covering

him and his wife were to melt, he'd be left in an
unfamiliar landscape. A landscape scoured by

years of frigid cold, a landscape fractured and heaved
by stress and pain and unbearable grief. And that

changed landscape, with or without ice, would be lacking
the very things most precious, sacred, and holy

to Eddie Madison — his manhood and his two
little girls. This is the force that compels Eddie

to action. This is the inescapable weight
that makes him go back to the house in the middle

of the night. When he sneaks into the house, it's so
cold, he can't stop shivering despite the sweatshirts

and the ski-mask he's wearing. It's so cold as he
creeps up the stairs, even his blood feels petrified.

Eddie stands over his sleeping wife, but it's so
dark he can barely see her. Eddie's hands are so

cold the girls whimper a little when he pulls them
from their beds. After he settles them in the back-

seat of the station-wagon, covered with blankets
and surrounded by their stuffed animals, the girls

fall back asleep, leaning heavily against each
other. He puts the suitcases and the laundry

basket of toys in the back. All that time, his wife
never wakes up. He puts the torn-up restraining

order on the kitchen table, next to the last
alimony and child-support check he'll ever

have to write. For the very first time in his whole
life, Eddie Madison — originally of

Scranton PA and soon to be formerly of
Deadwood, South Dakota — Eddie Madison does

not know who's going to cook his meals or wash his clothes
or trim his curly black hair when it hangs too long

down the back of his collar, and then his heart starts to
ache when he thinks of his wife tomorrow morning,

when she wakes up all alone, without their little
girls. But it's too cold for Eddie to hurt for long.

Before he leaves, he takes one last look around. The
sky is a strange grey color. There's no snow yet, but

there will be. Eddie can smell it in the air. He
waits to feel something, but all he can feel is cold.

After he starts the engine, he waits a few more
minutes, but nobody tells him not to go — not

his wife, not his heart, not even God. Eddie hits
all the green lights going through town, his two girls sleep

soundly in the backseat, and the whole freeway is
deserted. The further away Eddie drives, the

lighter the crushing weight on his chest feels, and that
surprises him. Eddie Madison always thought

that if he left his wife, some great, cataclysmic
disaster would occur. Like a flip in the earth's

magnetic field, like stars exploding in the sky,
like the earth's being assaulted and battered by

comet or meteorite impacts. But here he
is, driving away from her as fast as he can,

his two girls tucked safely away in the backseat,
despite her lawyer's threats and the judge's warnings,

and absolutely nothing happens. No earthquake.
No volcanic eruption. No big bang. Not even a whimper.

So all the scientists and the lawyers and the
priests were wrong. There is a God, and sometimes God loves

dinosaurs even more than He loves floods. Eddie
turns south when he hits Route 83. He doesn't

care where he goes, as long as it's warmer there. 'Cause
Eddie and his wife, they're about to become extinct.
ɑȝ

Auggie Vernon Gets Struck by Lightning

He wasn't out on a golf course during a freak
thunderstorm, he wasn't under the tallest tree
in the woods, and he wasn't on the roof fiddling
with the TV antenna. As a matter of
fact, when Auggie Vernon got struck by lightning, he

was sitting in his very own herringbone-tweed
Barca-Lounger, with the open Bible lying
on his lap and a can of beer in his left hand.
Nobody saw the blinding flash of light rip through
the roof of the house on Green Apple Lane. No one

heard the ominous rumble of thunder or felt
the sudden chill in the air. And absolutely
nobody heard Auggie Vernon scream. Because he
didn't. No, Auggie Vernon was struck dumb at the moment
of impact, so there wasn't any sound at all

except for some gurgling noises and the dull *cling*
of the beer can as it toppled to the floor. The
next morning, when Auggie's wife got home from her shift
at the hospital and found him, she didn't know
what had happened and he couldn't explain because

by that time Auggie Vernon was speaking in tongues.
Auggie's wife didn't even bother to take off
her nurse's uniform: she just shoved him into
the station-wagon and drove as fast as she could
back to the emergency room. The doctors were

stumped. No one had ever seen anything like it.
Not even Dr. Weiss, and he was from Brooklyn.
When Auggie Vernon finally stopped speaking in tongues
and started speaking English again, all he kept
saying was *Lightning!* but the doctors couldn't find

any marks that looked like burns, except for the scars
on his forearm from when he got drunk and bet he
could hold a lit cigarette to his skin longer
than anyone else. Besides, the Midwest had been
in the middle of a drought for the past three months,

so the doctors were pretty sure that they would've
noticed if it had rained in the past twenty-four
hours, and it hadn't. Still, there was something wrong
with Auggie Vernon. The mere fact that he wouldn't
let anyone pry the Bible out of his hand

was proof enough, even if everybody in
the emergency room hadn't heard him babbling.
For three days Auggie Vernon was without sight, and
he wouldn't eat or drink so they had to hook him
up to an IV-drip. After the English Lit

teacher from the high school came by the hospital
and heard Auggie shouting *Lightning! Lightning!* he said
Auggie'd had an epiphany, but since it was
still five months till Christmas, no one understood what
the teacher meant. By the time Auggie'd regained his

sight, he'd also stopped saying *Lightning!* but then all
he said was *Behold, O, ye despisers. Behold
and wonder. For I work a work in your days. A
work which ye shall in no wise believe, though a man
declare it unto you.* At least, that was pretty

much all he said till he overheard the doctors
recommending his transfer to the psych ward. Then
Auggie dropped all the King James vernacular and
started asking for meatloaf. Everyone agreed
it was a miraculous recovery. He

didn't protest when his wife took his Bible and
put it in the drawer of the bedside table, where
it remained even after he was discharged and
sent back home since everyone on the hospital's
staff was afraid to touch it. The Bible stayed in

that drawer until one of the janitors, wearing
three pairs of latex gloves, got brave enough to take
the Bible out of the drawer and put it into
the hazardous waste container, along with the
tainted gloves. By that time, however, Auggie had

himself a brand new Bible, with the words of Christ
in red, so he didn't care what they'd done with the
old one. He didn't even care when his wife gave
the old tweed Barca-Lounger to the Salvation
Army and bought him a new vinyl one. His wife

went back to work in the emergency room, on
third shift, just like always, and Auggie's favorite foods
were still meatloaf with loads of ketchup, and a side
of macaroni-and-cheese, so everyone thought
life was back to normal. Yes, Auggie Vernon was

hit by lightning in the middle of his living
room in the middle of a drought. He spoke in tongues
till he regained his sight, and he spoke King James till
Thursday, when the hospital serves meatloaf. Then he
went home and went on living his life exactly

as he had before. Except he started going to
church again. So it was just like the Monsignor
said: a miracle. But no one sees Auggie Vernon late
at night when he sits in his new vinyl chair in
the living room in the dark. No one sees how his

fingers fly over the pages of his brand new
Bible, with the words of Christ in red. No one sees
Auggie Vernon's eyes as his fingers rapidly
cover page after page. His eyes, glowing in the
dark. Glowing with a fierce and terrifying light.
CR

Eddie Madison and the Law of Gravity

Force without wisdom
falls of its own weight.

Horace
Odes 3.4.65

There is an unseen force in the universe that
is exponentially and immeasurably

greater than the invisible force which holds the
planets and moons in their unvarying orbits,

keeps comets travelling in calculable and
predictable elliptical paths, compresses

cosmic dust into incandescent, winking stars,
and prevents any object on the earth's surface

from escaping its invisible tethers to
float weightlessly in space. There is a weight that is

more cumbersome, massive, and ponderous than the
weight which results from gravity acting on mass,

a weight more substantial than pounds or kilograms
can measure, a weight heavier than an object's

inevitable attraction to the center
of the earth, a weight greater and heavier than

the constant, irresistible attraction of
each individual particle of matter

in the universe to every single other
particle. Eddie Madison knows this force, feels

this weight, every night as he stands over the beds
of his sleeping daughters, listening to the sound

of their breathing. Eddie Madison of Scranton,
Pennsylvania feels this weight, this force, in his chest,

in his guts, in his legs, until he wants to fall
to his knees, crawl into bed beside his little girls,

close his tired, swollen eyes and never open
them again. No one ever told him about this

invisible, irresistible force that has
determined his every movement since he first held

his daughters' squalling newborn bodies in his huge
hands and felt a breathlessness he couldn't explain.

No one ever articulated to Eddie
Madison of Scranton, PA, Albert Einstein's

General Theory of Relativity, which
views gravity as a property of space and

not as a force between bodies at all, which states
furthermore that as a result of the presence

of matter, space itself becomes curved, that bodies
will follow the line of least resistance among

those curves, that gravity is a consequence of
the curvature of space induced by the presence

of a massive object. But Eddie Madison
understands the pull and drag toward little bodies

who want you to lift them into your arms, settle
them against your great broad chest, the tops of their heads

just under your chin as you read them a bedtime
story. He understands the curvature of space

caused by tiny hands grasping your forefinger, by
butterfly kisses against your cheek at night, by

giggling and tickling and water-gun fights and by
the very sound of the word *Daddy*. Yes, Eddie

Madison understands everything there is to
know about weight and mass and force, and he's tried to

explain it all to his wife and his wife's lawyer.
He's tried to explain how the loss of his children

would thrust him into a void so dark and cold and
vast that, like a dead star, he would collapse under

the sheer weight and size and grief of it all. He's tried
to make them understand that without the weight of

his children to hold him firmly on the ground, he
might float, weightless and purposeless, into a space

deeper than the hell that awaits sinners and the
sewage of mankind. He's tried to explain that these

children are, at last, the bone of his bones, the flesh
of his flesh, the fruit of his seed. He's tried to tell

them that only God Himself can drive man out of
the Garden, and even then He can only keep

man out if He stations the cherubim with the
fiery ever-turning sword at the gate to

guard the way. But they won't listen. Instead, they throw
fierce and ugly words at him, words like *child support,*

alimony, and *supervised visitation,*
words that act on Eddie Madison with a force

great enough to move his bulky mass, great enough
to overcome inertia, self-doubt, and despair,

and move him to bundle up his children in the
middle of the night and drive so fast and so far

away that no one could ever find them, even
if Eddie hadn't taken the precaution of

changing all their names and their hair color besides.
Eddie Madison understands that doubling the

mass of an object doubles the force required
to overcome its inertia and bring about

a given acceleration, such as when the
case-worker from Children's Services leaves a message

on your answering machine to discuss your
wife's accusations and you suddenly see the

fiery, ever-turning sword. He understands
without having ever been told Newton's law which

states that for every action there is an equal
and opposite reaction. That's what the gun is

for. Yes, Eddie Madison of Scranton, PA,
understands that there is an invisible force

so great, an immeasurable weight so heavy,
that no man on earth could ever hope to escape

it. He feels that massive weight, that ponderous force,
every single night as he stands over the beds

of his sleeping children, tears running down his face
in predictable, calculable paths, his heart a

dead moon forever and irrevocably trapped
in an elliptical orbit around their sweet,

angelic faces. His love so great that it could
shatter every single law of the universe.

So heavy that it could crush the Serpent and blight
all the fruit in the Garden. So fierce that it could

re-shape the face of God Himself, fashioning it
in the image of his own haunted, hunted self.

&

The Lies Our Parents Tell Us

begin in childhood: *you're not dumb, you were not an
accident, the sight of you doesn't make us sick,*

we don't think you're ugly, and we swallow the lies,
with open hands and grateful hearts, because we're so

hungry, because the lies are all we have. The lies
our parents tell us get woven into our bones;

they form the raised scars over the cuts of childhood:
your nose isn't big, you're not fat, it doesn't hurt

*lightning bugs when you crush them onto your finger
to make a ring, that man just kills little black boys*

*and girls don't worry we'll protect you and keep you
safe we love you.* The lies grow with us, faithful

companions, more reliable than childhood friends
who break our toys or move away, warmer than our

favorite blankets, more dependable than lovers
who don't show up or don't call or stare blankly at

us from the arms of someone else. We trust the lies.
We know them. We take them into our own homes, wrap

them up in ribbons and bows, and give them to our
own children. And the lies go like this: your daddy

didn't lose his job because he stole money, Aunt
Lorna didn't kill herself, Uncle Max never

touched little boys or girls where he shouldn't have, we
never heard of anyone doing anything

with sheets but putting them on beds, democracy
is the only viable government, God made

us to have dominion
over all the creatures

on earth, the planet's ours.
Besides, it wasn't us.

&

Selling Your Brother

Am I my brother's keeper?

Genesis 4:9

Selling your brother isn't as difficult as
you might think, and he doesn't have to send up burnt

offerings of the first lambs of his flock, or wear
a coat of many colors, or interpret your

dreams at the breakfast table to fuel your fury.
It could be the way your mother gazes at him,

or the way your father chooses him to sit at
his right hand at the family gatherings. It could

be the way he bares his upper teeth, ever so
slightly, when he smiles at you, so you know the smile

is a pretense. Or it could be his beautiful
wife that makes you rage against him in the middle

of the night. Or it could be none of these things. You
don't need to justify your feelings: you don't plan

to kill him. Killing is so brutal, so savage.
This isn't the kind of man you are. Besides, you

don't want blood on your hands. You don't want his blood to
wither your crops or blight your herds. Far better to

sell him as a slave to a merchant traveling
to some distant land, better to sell him to the

highest bidder, better still to sell him and bring
back his blood-stained, multi-colored coat as proof of

his unfortunate demise. Of course, your father
will turn to you to handle your brother's end of

the business affairs. Your brother's land and crops and
animals will come to you since he has left no

children to inherit either his name or his
possessions. And then the beautiful, grieving young

widow will seek your strong shoulder in the long, dark,
lonely night. For solace, you understand. No one

will ever question your right to inherit the
most fertile cropland. Neither will they question your

obligation to beget children on the young
widow. When your cousins protest, no one listens

to their accusations: they're chronic malcontents.
Everyone else knows you have a right to these things.

It's not profit. It's inheritance. This is how
it's always been. This is how it should be. This is

the way God Himself has commanded that it be.
Then every night, after you have tasted of all that

was his, after you have glutted your hunger in
his bed, you can rise and gaze out over his lands,

Love In the Time Of Dinosaurs

his animals, his slaves, his woman, and you can
smile to yourself, there in the dark, for you know that,

given the chance to go back to that one fateful
day, that one day when the sun was shining too hot,

that day when his smile was too complacent or too
condescending, that day his wife's body was too

rounded and lush, given the chance to return to
that one bloody day, you know you would change nothing.

Absolutely nothing. Therein lies the sweetness.
Therein lies the honey and wine of your life. You

would do it all again, in exactly the same
way, just as you have re-lived it every night for

these many years. You smile as you return to your
bed, as you take his wife again in the dark, as

you hear your father weeping in the night. Thirty
pieces of silver or one — it doesn't matter.

It's the selling that counts.
And the selling is all.

portrait of the poet
as a woman

Love slays what we have been
that we may be what we were not.

St. Augustine

Should, Should Not

(after a poem by
Czeslaw Milosz)

A woman should not love a man, but if she does,
she should keep the child of their breath close to her heart.

A woman should not love a man, but if she does,
her house should be clean and tidy, her dinner-pots

full. Her garden should smell of lilacs and roses.
A man, when he loves a woman, should not use words

that are dear to her, or split open her heart to
find what's inside. She should never look over her

shoulder when crossing over his threshold (or so
our mothers teach us). When she crawls into his bed

at night, she may memorize his sleeping face as
a reminder of what will not last forever.
ൠ

Anniversary

Water steams in the yellow teapot. Dishes lean
precariously in the sink. The kitchen is

painted white, and has a scuffed wood floor. A dishtowel
is folded on the counter. The table sits near

a wall of windows. The wooden table is set:
two saucers, two teacups, two spoons, one knife, butter,

toasted bread, a sliced lemon sleeping in each cup.
In the center — real marmalade, bitter not sweet,

glistening in its jar. Beside it, in a brown
clay bowl, float rose petals. The spoons clink. One saucer

is chipped. The cat sleeps on the window sill. The blinds
are rolled up. A bare bulb is in the light overhead.
છ

A Cappella

Hurry: run back upstairs or you'll make your
father late. I'll hold your coat. Don't forget

your gloves. Remember how the cold burnt your
fingertips and made you cry in the night?

Here, wrap this scarf around your face and neck.
No, don't run, or you'll slip again. You know

how the rug slides on the wooden floor. A
good many faded rugs have been caught on

that sharp snag on the bottom of the door,
opened once to admit a stranger who

fogged all the windows, made Mommy cry, and
Daddy move out. What? Your gloves are hiding?

I know — you're too grown for them anyway
you're no baby. But daddy grows tired of

waiting and blasts the horn. You jump. Your best
friend lost something in the snow, your favorite

in the whole-entire-world-around. Here,
button up tight, and wear my mittens. Then

at least put your hands in your pockets. It
couldn't be found anywhere: the sky was

dark, getting darker, and I was calling
you for dinner. Now the house is getting

bigger, your favorite toys disappearing,
your friends becoming unreliable.

Daddy leans on the horn till you burst out
the front door, the new scarf unwrapping and

dragging through the dirty snow. I rest my
forehead against the closed door, wince at the

cold air rushing around the doorframe,
then kick the faded rug back into place.

Upstairs, the past wakes, wanders aimlessly
till it finds me in the kitchen, where it

gazes mournfully from the corners as
I re-heat last night's dinner. I chew each

bite at least twenty times, watch the clock's hands,
go to bed early. Last night, the nightmares

woke you again. I untangled you from
the blankets, dried your cheeks, tightened you in

my arms so you might hear the rhythm of
my own heart. Lost once in the deepest of

deep snows. Found again,
glittering with ice.

But not
by children.

ॐ

Haceldama

(Field of Blood)

And Judas, when he saw that he was
condemned, repented, and brought back
the thirty pieces of silver, saying, "I have
sinned in betraying innocent blood."

Matthew 27:3-4

I am standing by the Nile when seven
cows, sleek and fat, come out of the water

and browse in the grass. After them, seven
other cows, ugly and thin, come up out

of the Nile. The ugly thin cows devour
the sleek fat cows. Then I wake to find it

a dream. Leaving him sleeping, I search the
house for you, always finding it empty.

He never hears the cries, though they wake me
nightly. Frightened, my poems huddle at the

foot of the bed, hesitantly calling
to me, weeping that I don't recognize

them. Seeing the blood, I pass over you,
while, in some invisible vault, pieces

of silver glow. Repentance seldom brings
forgiveness. We must see to that ourselves.
ॐ

Portrait of the Poet as a Woman

Your second wife calls to say that the children get
ill after you bring them home Sunday night it must

be something they eat what do I feed them something
dreadful? She calls collect when she's away. If I

ask who's calling she says, *This is his wife*. If I
don't ask, she says, *This is his wife*. Sometimes she cries.

I want to feel for her pain, but loving a man
is penance enough. In the yellow tea kettle,

the water steams. Holding the phone to my ear, I
sit at the table with this morning's dishes. At

breakfast, your youngest son decided to hate the
toast, the jam, the world, me. I wanted to hold him —

the hands covering his face seemed so small, but his
older brother's stare fixed me, as if in a bad

photograph: off-center, one hand reaching out, the
other almost tipping my teacup, mouth open,

staring straight into the camera. Lot's wife stilled in
faltering. Pinned without wriggling to the wall. One

of the children slams the bathroom door. The water
steams, without whistling, in the yellow tea kettle.

Last night, one of your children cried out in sleep. The
wood of the hall was cool on my bare feet, and

my nightgown brushed my legs. You were already there
in his room. I stood near the open window and

listened to the hum of your deep voice, woven with
your child's answering sobs. The white lace curtains brushed

against my flattened belly, aching to be child-
swollen, to share you with something of me instead.

The water steams and she reminds me again that
I have moved into her house. I crumple some burnt

toast with my fingers. Outside, two brown sparrows hop
together in the dried leaves, talking bird-somethings.
ൟ

Among Children

The children will not sleep. Again. I lean against
their door, my hand brushing the wood, listening to

their faint, bird-song voices weaving webs between their
distant pillows. They never see me standing there.

Light beckons from under our bedroom door, where you
wait, reading in bed. I leave the children's voices,

close our bedroom window, and pull back the heavy
covers to crawl in beside you. Our fingers touch,

entwine. The children laughed at the breakfast table,
huddled over the cereal box, practically

empty, revealing some secret too precious for
my ears. *Hush touch touch.* Your whispered breath is welcome

on my breasts hot and heavy like the snow that the
children piled neatly in the back between the trees:

A fort, they said and went away giggling. I rushed
to the window to watch them trudging through snow, their

path ending in the haze beyond arms aching to hold
those too grown for such weakness. *Hush touch touch.* Yes, press

harder your mouth sweet on mine till I am able
to forget. This morning I wasn't able to

work: the children interrupted with an army
of friends, clattering, banging into the kitchen,

unsettling the cat, their boots leaving lakes on the
clean floor. The dim light softens the lines under your

eyes, my love. I hadn't quite noticed before the
echoes when I wait. Sometimes not long. Sometimes it

seems eternal. I like the feel of your skin; your
arms envelop me and let me lose myself where

no one will be able to find me, no matter
the looking. The eggs burnt in the pan. I stood there,

whisper-riveted, longing to share the empty
cereal box, my love collecting in Mason

jars. You don't see, and the children never notice.
Their trucks and cars are tumbling from bookcase-mountains,

their friends are spending the night, the snow is falling,
armies are moving seeking cat-hiding-places.

Much greater things call them. They have no time to take
from one who calmly regards smoking eggs in the

morning, unable to see things written ever-
so-plainly in the milk at the bottom of the

bowl. *Hush touch touch.* Yes, grind my nerves to shuddering
forgetfulness. The sheets are cool on our sweating

thighs. I like the feel of you sometimes you fill the
places razed by the smiles of golden-haired children.
ᏟᏜ

Holiday

Day followed day, and this and that
Seemed to be happening
As always, but through it all
Already loneliness was seeping.

Anna Ahkmatova

I pour myself another glass of wine, then lounge
on the wicker couch of the sun-porch, my bare feet

propped on an old milking stool, surrounded by texts
on the psychology of dreams. Late this morning

your first wife phoned, from where it is *not* raining: your
three children huddled around, chirping, while the cat

lapped milk from their cereal bowls. Outside the grey
rain shimmers, chanting the glossary of terms I

have yet to memorize. Thirteen-year-old Laura
eases into the Bentwood across from me, rocks

slowly. Her brothers pirouette onto the porch,
warbling *ninth-day-of-rain-it-never-rains-when-we're-*

in-school songs. I reward them with cookies, so they
dance away to the kitchen, crooning rain-songs for

each other. Last night the youngest stole two-thirds of
your gin-and-tonic, inquired of your mother:

Barbara, when you get drunk, do things look all different?
Beethoven drifts out from behind the door of the

room she's sharing with your daughter. Your typewriter
clacks as Laura strokes the cover of one of my

books. *Last night I dreamed I was swimming and couldn't
see land anywhere at all.* When her brothers

bounce onto the porch and propose rain-dancing, I
send them to you. Two minutes later, the back door

thuds, and muted squeals float back to us. Your clacking
chorus resumes. *I got real tired and called and*

*called to some man to save me but he was talking
to this mermaid. He didn't hear me so I guess*

I drowned. I present her one of the dream books; she
snuggles with it in a distant room. I wander

the summer cottage, open a second bottle
of wine, memorize your sons in glittering pools.

Last night I, too, dreamt: I was unrolling faded
oriental carpets onto scuffed wood floors. Three

sparrows fluttered down, whispering among themselves.
Their words swelled, joined hands, became the cars of a train

yanking away from an abandoned platform. My
legs lumbered after. The sparrows darted down,

snared the ticket from my extended hand, raced each
other to giggling clouds. The ticket escaped, spun

itself into a whirling dervish, scattering
the clouds and birds. Then I roamed through some crumbling old

house, breaking open all the curtains, unlatching
windows. You followed around behind, closing them.
☙

When The Animals Come Out

We could be doing anything — sitting at the
dinner table eating mashed potatoes, watching
commercials during the six o'clock news, stretching

our legs under the down quilt as we dream garden-
dreams — when the cages start to rattle. We could be
anywhere — on the porch, in the back yard, in the

laundry room — when their hungry growls and snarls tense us.
Suddenly they're looking out through our eyes. And what
they see is meat draped on bones. What they smell is fear.

What they want is blood. When our fingers twitch and curve,
our nails grow long, our teeth become much sharper.
We destroy the theory of evolution and

the new stoneware. After we stand upright again,
we tread warily around the house, sweep up the
broken dishes, mend the pillows, bandage our wounds,

avoid each other's eyes. Sometimes the animals
leave offspring. Mostly, though, they leave no survivors.
After each escape, we reinforce the bars on

the cages, dig deeper moats, hoard more stones in our
caves, eliminate visiting hours, change the
rules. And then the wind shifts. Our fingers twitch and yearn.
ଔ

The Toast

To God,
Who did not save us.

(after a poem by
Anna Ahkmatova)

Let's drink a toast to this dreadful old house, filled with
lost ghosts who come every night to roam around the

downstairs rooms, their limp ghost-hair straying across their
gloomy ghost-eyes. Let's drink to all the empty rooms

upstairs, meant for an absolute infestation
of tousle-haired, rosy-cheeked children, but housing

instead only walls of books, empty as our eyes
at the breakfast table when the drinks of the night

before have deserted us, leaving us only
each other. Let's toast the sons your scorned first wife hid

in Italy: your just and deserved punishment
for requiring someone younger, but for which you

never pardoned the new wife. Or let's toast that faint
stirring in my flattened belly — only once, long

before you were free to claim it. Let's raise our glass
to the clacking and clanking of your manual

typewriter in the middle of the night, and to
mine, which has been holding its electric tongue for

weeks, except to murmur the names in your frieze of
discarded women whenever I try to write

about something other than the space in the bed
between us, something other than our excuses

for not touching. And let's not forget to drink to
nineteen-year-old Seraphina in your fiction

writing class who called the house Saturday morning
and asked for you by first name. Let's drink to the God

who plucked us from our separate lives that last summer
your second wife visited her family in France,

molded us together in His callused palm, clamped
His heavy fingers like bars around us, and laughed.
❧

When Bitterness Is All We Have

Each morning, our eyelids scratchy, the curtains closed,
we chew dry toast and swallow runny scrambled eggs

as we gloat over the new headlines: *Serial
Killer Reveals Latest Victim, Foreign Cities*

Destroyed by Bombs, War Imminent. We sigh as we
turn the pages, saying, *We tried to tell them they*

*wouldn't listen they never do it's a shame but
it's all their fault we warned them.* We sip our coffee

black, no sugar. Over lunch in the restaurant,
at our usual table, a bare bulb in the

light overhead, we detail our children's lazy
spouses, their poor salaries, their mounting debts, their

gambling, their drinking, their infidelities, their
own wayward, rebellious children. We nod. *They*

*deserve every bit of suffering for the way
they treated us after all we did for them those*

ungrateful those selfish beasts. We pass the bread and
stare, commenting on the neighboring diners. Nights,

people are too busy to spend time with us: this
son has a scout meeting, that daughter has baton practice

or a piano recital, old college friends
are spending the weekend, someone has a cold, the

dog just tracked mud over the kitchen floor. We smile
wisely to ourselves. We remind each other how

sorry they'll be and how much they'll miss us when we're
gone. When I tell you about my work, you doze off.

When you try to explain life's complexities, I
yawn. Dishes get slammed in the sink. The radio

gets turned louder. The space in the bed between us
grows. When we can't sleep, we stay up late to watch old

black-and-white movies. We sit in the dark. At the
end, when the hero sweeps the one true love of his

life into his arms promising *forever and*
ever truly deeply faithfully till death do

us part we look across the room at each other,
faint and distant in the flickering light, and smile.
છ

Holding Our Hearts In Our Hands Like Rock

What strength have I, that I should endure?
Is my strength the strength of rock?

Job 6:11-12

It never begins the way you might expect, this
shifting and cracking of the earth beneath your feet,

this terrible movement that destroys earth, buildings,
lives. The tremors start deep underground: days, weeks, months,

even years before they erupt at the surface
of our lives, but no one notices until it's

too late. It happens in the night, in the cold and
lonely dark of night. It may not even wake you,

so deep is your sleep, but when you do awake in
the morning, you wake to a new landscape. A cold,

unfamiliar, frightening landscape. Your mother's gone.
You don't know why, but no one speaks her name again.

Night after night, you cry in your bed, but no one
comes to dry your tears. The foundation of your heart

has buckled: you'll never be the same. For many
years after, you do your best to make the earth move

again, to shift your life back to the way it should
be: you jump off the crossbar of the swing-set, you

swallow all the aspirin in the child-proof bottle,
you lower your bare wrist to the jagged edge of

window glass. But the earth stays still. The sun shines as
it always does. Only the metallic taste in

your mouth and your nervous jumping at strange noises
remind you that your new life is not the same as

the old, that this new landscape isn't on any
maps. You grow up, fall in love, marry, have children

of your own. You learn to laugh again. You don't mean
to, but, yes, there are days when you feel quite happy.

That's when it happens. But not like you'd expect. No,
the sky doesn't darken at noon. Birds don't fall, stunned,

from the cloudless sky. The sun doesn't stand still in
the middle of the day. It doesn't happen like

that. It happens like this: the earth under your feet
moves. That's all. It simply moves. Perhaps it moves by

mere centimeters. Perhaps it moves only the
width of a strange lipstick mark on a shirt collar,

only the length of a phone number on a scrap
of paper hidden between the socks in a drawer.

It seems to you that the earth cannot move in this
way. Not in this random, careless, stupid way. But

Love In the Time Of Dinosaurs

the earth has, indeed, moved. The foundation of your
life has shifted, trembled, cracked. Your spouse pours bleach on

your collar but says nothing. Your children squeal and
laugh as they run through the sprinkler in the backyard.

The cat purrs as it rubs against your ankles. The
neighbor's lame dog barks when you get the mail. But none

of it's the same. You're not the same. You've finally done
it. You made the earth move. Now you'll have to gather

up the wreckage, the debris of your life, and hold
those fragments, heavy and broken, in your hands. You

don't know this now, but that weight will be the hardest
weight you have ever known. The hardest weight of all.

Like rock.
Like love.
ଓ

Group portrait: During Eclipse

Things do not change:
We change.

Henry David Thoreau

Group Portrait: During Eclipse

Anna
(Hungary)

There she stands, layers of brown and grey wool in a
field of snow while, on the horizon, three horsemen

appear. Their white breath and the frantic snow form a
hollow frame for the dark riders. She watches their

snow-slowed movements. Too late, she grasps their intentions.
They speak to her in a language that leaves marks on

pale skin. Afterward, bruised and lying on her back,
she stares at the cold, clear sky: blue, no clouds.

Geneviève
(France)

She sits at the table with the breakfast dishes,
staring out the windows, a damp towel folded near

her arm. In her hand, an unsigned letter, with a
local postmark, no salutation: *You must know*

your husband and I love each other. We want to
be together. The yellow tea kettle whines while

outside in the yard the children and their friends shoot
each other, falling down dead in the crisp, dry leaves.

Sophie
(Greece)

She presses her hand to the small of her aching
back as she rests from putting away the laundry.

Over the shower, she hears his faint singing. In
his top dresser drawer, between folded clothes, she finds

a picture — his first wife. She stares at it a long
time before she goes to the mirror. There, she holds

the photograph up under her chin, to see both
faces — both of his wives — at the same time. Behind

her taut belly, the child
moves, its limbs fluttering.

Isabella
(Spain)

They swim on a night with no stars, without
bathing suits, her wavy hair wet down the middle

of her back. On the hills above them, a lone train
passes, its yellow windows their only light. On

the train, men smoke cigarettes as they stare out at
the darkness. Behind her, he presses his body

to hers as he breathes against her throat: *Isabel.*
Again and again: *Isabel.* When at last she

opens her light eyes and
stands, the train is long gone.
಴

Penelope to Ulysses

(on their first night together after his return)

Of course, I believe you. Why should I imagine
you with any other woman these twenty years
you've been wandering? They say that the gods themselves

wander, that the gods themselves lose their way, yet their
wives open their arms, their hearts, their beds. The wives of
the gods swallow those honeyed words after all that

wandering, so who am I not to? Though I do
wonder why you waited so long to speak, why you
waited to reveal yourself, why you pretended

to be a beggar. I know. I heard what you said —
you had to clear your house of those dogs sniffing at
me for years while I waited for the man who was

my husband. You said you had to make sure all had
gone well while you were away. But I know what you
meant. You asked if our son grew into a man in

your absence, but what you really meant is did I
allow men to visit my apartments late in
the evening or for an hour in the afternoon.

Love in the Time of Dinosaurs

Long ago I learned to steel myself against the
words of men. Yes, dear, of course I believe you. Why
shouldn't I? Though I do wonder how you could have

managed to resist the charms of that lush nymph. You
know — the one who swore, in her devotion, that you
should never die or grow old all your days with her.

I believe you, though your eyes, when you spoke my name
with your weight up on taut arms, your eyes were cold and
pale. As if they had looked on things I could never

dream. I believe you. Though your eyes on the curves of
that young serving maid at dinner didn't glint so
cold and grey. After dinner, I came back to tell

you how good it would be to go to my bed and
be able to rest. How good it would be not to
spend the darkness untangling the lies of the light.

How good it would feel, after so much waiting, your
hard body next to mine. You didn't see me, but
your eyes on her weren't cold or hard. Yes, my darling,

I believe you. I believe you. Why must you ask
until there are tears, until they roll crookedly
down the face that is not the face you left? Not the

face you dreamt of while you never ever slept with
anyone all those years away from my side as
I made, unmade, made again our lives together.

As I waited for the stranger who sleeps now in
my bed. As I waited for the stranger whose dark
back is scarred with pale quarter-moons in a pattern

that might almost fit my woman's hand if I dared
to place my fingers there. If I dared not believe
the man who is my husband. It's a coldness though.

More than a cold and aching pain. Like crushing back
into my ancient shriveled womb the child that I
heaved forth screaming so many barren years ago.

ᘓ

The Strength of Stones

As the summer of my sixteenth year approached, the
village women began to give me advice, as

I made my rounds with the basket of eggs, on how
to get a husband, who would put roof-slates over

my head and children in my belly. All spring then,
I dutifully followed their suggestions: I

searched for a radish-root forked in two, with each side
shaped like a person. I wrapped a sliver of my

father's cousin's wedding bread in one of the thin
handkerchiefs from my dowry and kissed it three times

before slipping it under my pillow. I found
seven smooth pebbles, exactly the same size, and

breathed on them seven times before tossing them quick
over my left shoulder on the eve of the last

day of spring planting. But the summer passed without
promises. Then, as autumn neared, some faraway

conflict began to steal the villages' young men.
Before they departed, they presented words and

love-tokens to their local sweethearts, to ensure
their safe return. Even your eyes were bright with an

unfamiliar fire: I had to use my last charm.
At midnight on the eve of the saint's day, just as

my father's second wife had instructed me, I
crept out of bed and knelt before the hearth to dry

the magic ingredients: marigold flowers,
sweet marjoram, wild thyme, wormwood. While I rubbed them

into the simmering honey, I prayed as she'd
taught, *Saint of Love, Love Saint, be kind to me. In dreams*

let me my true love see, and anointed myself
three times before crawling back into bed, waiting

for the sweetest of all girls' dreams — the one which would
reveal my future husband. *Nadia!* you hissed,

Nadia! and your whispering scattered my dreams.
Your voice hovered over the wheeze and snore of

my stout father, over the anxious sighs of my
sleeping stepmother, over the slap of bare feet

on the cool stone floor, over the metallic click
of the latch, and the scrape of the door's swollen wood.

Nadia! Come out! In the moonlight your hair glowed
almost white. Your rucksack loomed large and black behind

you. Night air rushed cold through my thin gown. *Albert,*
I whispered, and clutched the frayed shawl tighter to my

breast. *Nadia, I'm off to fight the Czar,* you said,
and the lips that chafed my cheek were cool and dry as

fallen leaves. *When I return,* you said, *we'll marry.*
Your blond hair strayed across your forehead. Your rucksack's

straps were dark against the shoulders of your white shirt.
Will you wait for me? you asked, though you had never

breathed my name against my throat, or woven strands of
my thick hair with yours to pin upon my breast, or

crushed caraway between your fingers and rubbed the
scent on mine. *Nadia, will you wait?* you whispered,

though we had never tied a white ribbon to our
wrists and jumped over the threshold, or split apples

and spilled their seeds around the feet of our parents,
or clasped soil from our fathers' lands while the village

elders poured oil and water over our clenched hands.
Will you wait for me? you said, though I had never

stitched an elegant *A* beside an intricate
N on the borders and hems of the linen, or

baked a dense loaf of double-crusted bread to eat
with preserves at your family's table, or rubbed cloves

of garlic with onions into a paste for your
family's stew, or accepted a bracelet of reeds

for my left wrist, or, with my fingers in your hair,
pulled you down to lie beside me in the cool grass.

Only this — *Will you wait for me?* A tremulous
sigh escaped my lips, and you pressed a bleached stone the

size of an egg in my open palm: *I plucked this
as a boy from my grandfather's stream. It's for luck.*

You gazed at the smoothed white of your childhood, lying
in my cupped hand, and I gazed at your eyes and lips

showered by moonlight. Only your hesitant voice
after I had simmered and stirred, fasted and prayed,

anointed and dreamed. Then only my mute nod in
response to this miraculous midnight courtship.

Marjoram, marigold, wormwood, thyme. *You will wait
for me, won't you?* Oh, yes. Your boots trudged down the dirt

path, the night's silence wrapped around you as tightly
as the ribbons mothers wove through the braids of a

new bride. The stone was heavy in my hand. The wind
tangled my curls and flattened my nightdress to my

trembling legs. My shawl escaped my hand and fluttered
to the ground, scattering leaves, while you strode to the

war to end all wars, which would take your brothers' lives
and steal the light from your eyes, but you never once

glanced back. So you didn't feel my heart's frantic dance,
nor hear the bittersweet tune my blood trilled to yours.
℞

Counting the Thunder

Storms coming, the old woman hissed to us when we
went to fetch water from the well. Oona had been

dancing her corn-doll in the dust of the dry road
ahead of us, but she scrambled back to my side

when she heard the old woman's voice. The old one stepped
out of the field and leaned closer to us. *Didst thou*

see the moon last reaping-day? she said. *Out at*
high-sun. No good comes of it. Oona tried to

hide herself behind my skirts. *We knows thee,* said the
old one, pointing her bone walking-stick at me. *Born*

Lammas Eve three and ten harvests past, the first day
of the Great Storms. Oona looked up at me. *We knows*

thee. Thou seest, the old woman said, nodding. *And*
storms know thee, too, Daughter. Then she limped into the

field's shadows as the wind banged the bucket against
my leg. Oona would not approach the well. We ran

home and told our brother the old woman's words. He
snorted with laughter, gripped his cow-herding stick, and

boldly trudged ahead of us, boasting the vast
dangers that awaited the old witch dream-teller

if she returned. As I drew water for the house,
I kept glancing around. Oona clutched my skirts. Our

brother brandished his battle-blade, shouting, *Come for
me, Old One.* His stick cracked against the hard ground, his

wheat-colored hair a helmet against the clouded
sky. *Girls,* he sniffed in disdain after she failed to

return and answer his challenge, disappointed
he'd been unable to catch glory. By the late

evening meal, he and Oona have forgotten it
all. I say nothing to Papa, but I cannot

eat. Mama presses her lips to my forehead and
sends me straight to bed. But I don't close my eyes. Soon,

Oona crawls under the feather-cover and is
dream-breathing. The skies flash day-light, then plunge into

deeper night-shades. Mama says if we count from the
moment we see the storm-light till the thunder growls,

we'll know how many years of full crops, how many
years of apple-cheeked babes and strong young men before

the dread-years return. The light cracks. I hold Oona
close, my cheek against her hair. The light comes again.

Before I unbend my
first finger, thunder speaks.
oR

Ahab's Wife

Must ye then perish,
and without me?

Herman Melville
Moby-Dick

Each night she stands in the open doorway, her hair
frenzied by the wind, a shawl around her shoulders.
After she bolts the door, she wanders through the dark,

empty rooms. As she passes the cradle, the child
whimpers, so she gathers him to her breast, then coos
him to anxious dozing. While he dreams, she gazes

down at him, brushes his soft cheek with her fingers.
She looks away, out the window, remembering
herself as a young child, still an orphan, even

in her uncle's house. One night in summer, she threads
blue ribbons in her dark hair, then lurks around the
parlor, hoping to glimpse the tall, gaunt visitor.

Her uncle sees her, swears, orders her to bed, but
the other says, *Ah, Sarah,* as he reaches for
her, as he lowers his tall, thin frame so that their

faces meet. Delicately, she places her cool
fingers on his cheek, on the scar. His palm brushes
over her thick dark hair, snags one of the blue silk

ribbons. Behind them, the fire spits. With the child in
her lap, she remembers another version of
herself — the young wife waiting on a wind-battered

wharf, clutching her son, as the murmuring crowd grows
still, as it divides itself like the biblical
sea. From the crowd's midst, he lurches forward, paler

than the scar on his cheek or the new-fashioned
leg. She holds up the child. *Jacob,* she says, offering
their son to him, but the child shrieks and grasps her neck.

He limps home alone. She stands and stares a long time
at the sea — his sea. Every night after dinner,
he paces his study, his new leg tapping on

the wooden floor, until he walks himself to sleep,
until he collapses in one of the large chairs.
Every night, alone in their vast bed, she hugs the

pillows as she curses her own hesitation,
her own trembling. Then one night, his loud cries wake her.
She rushes to him, kisses his clenched fists, bends his

writhing, shuddering form to her warm body, chants
his name until his eyes see her, until his voice
coughs out her name, until, with an animal sob,

his mouth chafes hers. Every night after that, they are
together. On their last night, she jolts awake in
their abandoned bed. She discovers him in the

child's room, over the cradle. Behind him, the wind
rattles the windows. The moonlight haloes his greyed
hair, glows on the child's face, glares on the new leg. She

Love In the Time Of Dinosaurs

calls to him, but he stays still. She grips his arm through
the coarse cloth. He doesn't move. Tomorrow his ship
will wrench away. She opens her eyes, aches with the

longing for him. It's too long since he's been
with her, too long before the sea surrenders him
to her again. The wind swells, heaves snow from the roof

with a thud. She lays the child in her bed, secures
the blanket on either side of him, drags her long
fingers through his dark curls, kisses his cheek, and sighs.

She waits by the window, gazing at his dark and
heaving sea as, all around them, pale-blue snow swirls,
climbs into steep crests, collapses upon itself.
೫

Blood Songs

For the past month, in the midst of winter in the
Midwest, for hours each morning and evening,

in sunlight and in lamplight, with charcoal pencils, inks,
and pastels, I've been sitting beside the rented

hospital bed where you lie unconscious, drawing
your hands: palm up, palm down, folded, emptied, filled. Now

I have hundreds of hands, but none of them fits my
painting: *Grandfather Coming to America.*

They're good hands, these hundreds of hands I've drawn, and they
recognizably portray your narrow wrists and

long fingers, but all of these drawn hands are far too
feeble to be yours, too flimsy to have wrenched a

seventeen-year-old boy from his small village in
the Old Country and hauled him across an ocean

to some immense city in the New World, too slight
to have persuaded a wide-hipped girl with dark braids

coiled over her ears to desert the stout peasant
heritage of her parents and their people to

follow a man who wasn't even her husband
to a country that was lifetimes from her birthplace

with a language not her own. No, these hands I've drawn
couldn't have lured a virgin to journey alone

to a name on a map where a boy claimed he'd be
waiting for her. Except for your hands, the painting

is complete, though I have placed you and Grandmother on
the same boat: you, standing with your legs wide apart,

your face turned westward, your arms extended so that
the hands grip the boat's icy iron rails, and her,

with her heavy braids and solid hips, winter shawl
around her neck and wide shoulders, gazing up at

you, your eyes narrowed and your hair blown back by the
fierce wind. In the painting, her full lips are parted,

but you haven't heard her words because she's spoken
in the language of distant mountains and memories

willingly abandoned, and not in the language
of the hopes and dreams which beckon you across the

ocean. It's a good portrait, although it doesn't
show the explosion of scar near your left shoulder

where an enemy bullet pierced you in the war
that ended your brothers' lives but not all wars. It's

a good painting, although it doesn't reveal the
ribs cracked during the escape from the prisoner

of war camp when you hurled yourself over the wire
and into the woods, although it doesn't show you

limping home to your village and finding instead
fields of corpses. It's a good picture, its sea blue,

green, and gold. It's a good portrait of you, except
for the missing hands. In paint, your arms extend with

locked elbows to the wrists and there, a turpentined
emptiness mocks my efforts. And so, here I sit,

but without any drawing implements. Tonight,
I will not draw. Tonight, I will not speak any

language except the language of hands. Tonight, my
fingers will read the Braille of your ancient hands. My

fingers will weave themselves with yours until the warp
of your life and the weft of mine become one heart,

until your skin surrenders and speaks to mine in
that lost language, until your old bones dry, become

hollow, and whistle me the tunes of your childhood,
until, at last, the wide peasant palms and long paint-

stained fingers of my young woman's hands inherit
the elusive past that blood sings only to blood.
႙

Fireflies

When dusk falls, the first fireflies wink and dance near the
bedroom window. *Marie, Marie,* my cousin laughs,
seizing them with one hand. No one else is so good

at it. *Marie, Marie,* he sings and I come, pale
braids over my shoulders. *Here's a ring for you,* he
says, crushing the bug just as its body flickers so

it stays gold. He tears off the head, presses the bright
gold body onto my finger. I hold out my
hand. We admire it. Those I'd trapped in a jar are

dead in the morning. I empty them in the grass.
I'm sorry, Marie, my cousin stutters, twisting his hat.
Mama says we couldn't have. I can't explain over

father's shouting and uncle's cursing. My aunt faints.
The opera records drone in the living room. I
like the music though I don't understand the words.

They drift through the darkness, perching on the end of
my bed, awaiting invitations. *Go away,* I
order them. He doesn't understand words either.

I slap him. The look on his face joins the words at
the bottom of the bed. My cousin introduces
him to the others. They all shake hands. The words wink,

giggle. *How did you like Marie?* my cousin asks.
I bury my face in the pillow. The scent of your hair
surfaces. I turn over, memorize the ceiling. *Hold*

on, Marie; it will only last a moment. The
doctor may be a German. I tell him my hair
is naturally this color. He shoves my knees

further apart. I will put enmity between you and the
woman. *Just a few minutes more, Marie.* I don't
answer the doctor's questions. I forget my crime

was shared. I concentrate on the strain of
my fingers gripping the edge. A voice calls to me
from the midst of fire. I feel myself falling.

Marie, Marie, the children next door chant. They
grab fireflies — *lightning bugs,* they insist. I teach
them how to make rings. They puff like bullfrogs with the

secret, carrying it around with them for months. One
stumbles in her excitement, skinning her elbow and
knee. When the record ends, the words start to grumble.

If I don't go in, they'll come searching for me. They
don't trust me. They're dancing in the bedroom when I
get back. *Don't be a wallflower, Marie.* After

I crawl into bed, you join me. *Shhh,* you whisper.
The words start snickering. You shove them out of the
room. They crouch at the edge of the door, eavesdropping.

Marie, you breathe against my throat, *Marie.* I don't
want words: cast them out with the others. Bolt the door.
Marie, Marie, marry me. The jump-rope stings the

sidewalk. It is too late for children. I recognize
the rhythm, but not the song. *Cinderell-uh, dressed
in yell-uh, ran upstairs to kiss a fell-uh, made*

*a mistake, kissed a snake, how many doctors did
it take?* The doctor looks over my knees at me.
This can't keep happening, you know. I admit nothing.

Love in the Time of Dinosaurs

You're an intelligent woman. I say nothing.
A woman in the next room moans. The doctor gives
me a look. I turn my face to the whitewashed wall.

He shakes his head. The blue-and-white nurse frowns.
Marie, Marie, marry me. Now you are singing
to the jump-rope. *Marry me, Marie, Marie.* The

words hear. They roll on the floor, holding their sides.
Turn up the record to drown them. *Never mind,* you
say, pressing me against the bed with the weight of

your breath. *Am I too heavy?* you ask. No. Only
at times. I shiver. *What?* you ask. Nothing. *But
I need you,* he tells me. I am silent. His

youth shatters, a bottle of wine against wood. I
slip away. He cannot move. I lie with you in
afternoon sun, imagine your wife, with your

arms around me. I cry in the bathroom so you
won't see, turn on water full-force so no one hears.
The words are crumpled in sleep on the floor in the

hall. The touch of our bodies is such sweet music,
I want to join in at the chorus. Fireflies dance,
explode inside my head. The doctor scrapes off thin

plastic gloves. Your wife watches you when you're
home, lingers in the room when someone telephones.
The bedroom's as dark as Egypt. I crush pillows

to my chest, force them behind my back. I don't fool
myself for long. *Marie, Marie, hold on tight.* The
floor rushes up, opening its arms to catch me.
&

Hearts,
The Game

(after Hoyle's)

Players: a king and queen of the same suit.
Three or four players may participate

in rotation, but only two play at
a time. The vital consideration

in selecting alternate partners is
to avoid loving those alternates: this

will forestall quarrels that arise from any
feelings that favoritism is shown.

If possible, young or unguarded hearts
should be avoided since they cause trouble:

pass them if you can afford to do so.
With pale hair and in a cream suit, Henry

leans against the white-washed wall of a bar
somewhere. The beer warms in his hand. A girl

of perhaps Spanish descent sways among
smoke-wreathed tables, red shoes brighter than the

gold in her ears. Her white blouse swells damply
with the pounding of the music. Her long

hair is almost lank from exertion. She
feels him watching, longing. She tosses her

hips, snaps her fingers. He drinks, imagines
he could tell her things he has done that are

best forgotten. The music stops. He drains
the glass. She wipes moisture from her forehead,

her top lip. With her head slightly down, she
looks at him. He takes a step toward those eyes.

When the play first begins, each player is
intent on avoiding any and all

hearts. But once a player has taken a
heart, he does not care how many more he

may have to take: his only chance then is
to win all the hearts himself, whether or

not he should decide, at some later point,
to discard any of his possessions.

The water of the shower pounds. Katharine
closes her eyes, recalls when Henry rushed

home to her, frantic for her touch. He would
turn in sleep, whisper her name. She would wake,

smile at the new gold on his finger, on
hers. With dry eyes, she shuts off the water.

Some old-fashioned players feel that so long
as a player does not actually cheat,

he should not be bound by any code of
ethics. Most, however, feel that there is

a limit beyond which one should never
venture in misrepresenting his hand,

though this limit is apt to be somewhat
arbitrary and subtle, according

to the individual wives concerned.
A girl's voice over the telephone claims

to love him. Henry steps out of the bath,
wraps a towel 'round. Katharine replaces the

receiver. Humming, he pours tea. She dries
her hands on the dishtowel, folds it, lays it

on the counter. A slice of lemon falls
into his cup. The phone rings. She leaves the

room. He answers. Steam rises from the sink.
There must be a new deal to all of the

players if at any time one hand is
found to have too many and another

too few, as when a wife says she knows. Their
room wavers in the afternoon sun. She

memorizes everything: dark curls, green
jacket, muscled back. She will tell Henry

every detail about this boy. He drags
his jeans on, his back turned, and promises

to call her next Wednesday. The door slams. She
roams the house, her vodka-and-tonic in

hand. The downstairs mirror surprises her:
she shatters her glass against her image.

Love In the Time Of Dinosaurs

Proved or admitted errors in the score
of any player may be corrected

at any time before the end of the game
as long as the majority of

players agree. An understanding which
develops between original

partners is not unethical if their
alternates are also informed of this.

Katharine unlocks the front door, sneaks toward the
stairs. Light floods the far room. She turns. Henry

is sitting, legs extended, arms across
the back of the sofa, hair disheveled,

scotch nearby. She raises her chin. He pours
another drink, crosses to the hallway,

largo. She leans back on the banister.
He sees her hand, sets down his glass, tugs the

ring from his own finger, drops it into
the dark liquid. They glare at each other.

Partnership is contrary to the game's
spirit, so even when a husband and wife

are in the same game, they should regard each
other as opponents. They should never

intentionally break rules, however,
even when willing to pay penalties,

though it is permissible to force bids.
Still dressed, Henry lies on her bed, all the

pillows behind his back, swirls the ring in
his glass, bottle on the table. Wearing

a white robe, toweling moisture from her hair,
she comes in, stopping when she sees him. He

doesn't look up. Katharine dries her hair a
few minutes more, picks up a comb from the

dresser, drags it through. Henry puts his glass
down, comes over behind her, presses his

stubbled cheek next to hers. She stops combing.
When Henry grips her shoulders, Katharine pulls

away. He holds her arms, arches her back.
She watches him in the mirror: his mouth

to her throat. Her eyes close. She leans into
him, then jerks away. Henry turns her head,

tightens his fingers in her wet hair, his
mouth open on hers. Katharine wraps her arms

around his neck, drags him closer to her.
When his hands slip under the robe, the robe

falls. The ring glitters in the emptied glass.
The object of the game is to win.
౪

Speaking for the Dead

Every morning in the kitchen, from eight-thirty
to eleven, I piece together the scraps of
other people's lives. People I have never known

come to me, like frightened children in a new school,
bearing the scraps of their lives in heavy cardboard
boxes: birth certificates, marriage licenses,

death certificates, daguerreotypes, photographs.
I sort through the precious pieces until I am
able to stitch the names and faces into a

solid fabric, like an heirloom quilt that can be
passed from generation to generation. This
morning, trapped in the house by rain, my young daughter

comes to my office, a black-and-white photograph
in her hand. *No,* I tell her, *it's no one we know.*
She looks disappointed. I bought the photograph

from a vendor at a flea market — he'd bought it
at an estate sale. How those eyes haunted me: in
the photograph, faded and cracked with age, two men,

with dark hair and pale, almost white, eyes, stand beside
each other. Each rests one hand on the shoulder of
a dark-eyed woman, seated in front, between them,

her hands in her lap, her lips slightly parted as
if she has just said something which has made the men
look at her instead of at the photographer,

all their mouths captured forever in faint, half-smiles.
On the back of the photograph, in spidery
black ink, are three names: *Ernest, Vivienne, Jacob.*

No, I tell my daughter, *I don't know which is Jacob.*
And yet what lives I've invented for the three of
them — Jacob and Ernest are brothers, both in love

with Vivienne, who, caught in this moment, thinks she
will never have to choose between the two of them.
Or this — Ernest and Vivienne are devoted brother and sister,

both of them desperately, passionately in love
with Jacob. Only Vivienne is permitted
to love Jacob, so Ernest stands by, forever

longing. Ernest loves Vivienne for keeping his
secret. Both of them love Jacob every day for
the rest of their lives. Or this — both men are in love

with Vivienne; each belongs to someone else. Years
later, discovering the photograph, one of
their spouses or children tries to efface the name

Vivienne. Or this — two brothers and a sister
who have fled Russia's icy wastelands and pogroms
have come to America to start new lives. They

take this picture to commemorate their escape.
Or this — three siblings who've lost all their relatives
in the gas chambers of the Holocaust have been

reunited. They gaze in hesitant wonder
at their thin, trembling bodies, at their pale faces,
almost unrecognizable. Three young people,

barely more than children, have escaped the war or
the poverty, the hatred or the despair in
their village or in their homeland. This is the place

they'll start again, together, in peace. *This one is
Jacob,* says my daughter, pointing, and I see that
she's right. With the confidence and certainty of

childhood, she tells me what I've been struggling years to
learn. *This one is Jacob,* she says, before she runs
to tell her two older brothers, weaving with her

words one fine strand of the rope that moors us to the
past, that fine and tenuous rope that allows us
to open our mouths and speak, at last, for the dead.
ℂ੪

About Alexandria

Alexandria Constantinova Szeman

Critically acclaimed & award-winning author, Alexandria Constantinova Szeman (formerly writing as "Sherri" Szeman because her 1st editor told her that her name "wouldn't fit on the book cover," & wanted an "easy" first name to go with her "hard" last name) began as a poet before she started writing novels, short fiction, and creative writing books.

Szeman has Ph.D.'s in Creative Writing and in English & Comparative World Literatures. Her dissertation, *Survivor: One Who Survives* (University of Cincinnati, 1986) was a collection of original poetry, all of which were accepted or published by university & literary journals before her dissertation defense. While in graduate school, her poetry was awarded numerous prizes, including The Elliston Poetry Prize (several times) & The Isabel and Mary Neff Creative Writing Fellowship.

Her first novel, *The Kommandant's Mistress*, on the Holocaust from multiple points of view and perspectives, was chosen as one of *The New York Times Book Review*'s "Top 100 Books of the Year" (1993). It was also awarded the University of Rochester's (NY) prestigious Kafka Prize "for the outstanding book of prose fiction by an American woman" (1994), and Central State University's (OH) Talmadge McKinney Research Award (1993).

Originally published by HarperCollins (1993) & HarperPerennial (1994), the novel has been sold to publishers in 10 foreign countries and translated into French, Spanish, Russian, Lithuanian, Danish, Swedish, Norwegian, among others. It was republished by Arcade (2000) & was optioned for film (though funded, it was never made).

Her second novel, *Only with the Heart,* on the devastating effects of Alzheimer's on a family, is on the recommended reading lists of Alzheimer's Associations nationwide. Originally published by Arcade (2000), the Revised & Expanded, 12th Anniversary Edition contains new scenes with updated medical treatment/medications for Alzheimer's, as well as new legal definitions and statutes regarding assisted suicide.

Her third novel, *No Feet in Heaven,* about two brothers and their female cousin who decide to attain fame by hunting down a notorious serial killer themselves, won praise from several NY editors before it was accepted by a New York Trade House; unfortunately, that House was purchased by a larger NY Trade House: the editor was then laid off, and the book "rejected."

The titular story in her award-winning collection of short stories, *Naked, with Glasses,* won Third Prize in *Story Magazine*'s "Seven Deadly Sins Contest" (1995), and the manuscript won the Grand Prize in the

UKA Press [United Kingdom Authors Press] 2007 Annual International Writing Competition.

Her two poetry collections, *Love in the Time of Dinosaurs* and *Where Lightning Strikes: Poems on the Holocaust,* both contain critically acclaimed & award-winning poems. Each volume includes several poems from her dissertation, *Survivor: One Who Survives* (University of Cincinnati, 1986). The poems have won several prizes, including University of Cincinnati's Elliston Prize (anonymous competition; 1983, 1984, 1985), an Honorable Mention in the Chester H. Jones Poetry Foundation National Poetry Competition (1985), Michigan State University's *The Centennial Review* Michael Miller Award for Poetry (1985), an Honorable Mention in *Writer's Digest* National Writing Competition (1980), and The Isabel & Mary Neff Fellowship for Creative Writing (1984-85). Both volumes were unanimously accepted for publication by all outside readers of UKA Press [United Kingdom Authors Press] in 2004.

Szeman is currently completing her latest novel, as well as revising her memoir (about growing up with a mother who practiced Munchausen's by Proxy), and is about to publish several creative writing exercise books, including an e-book version of her classic *Mastering Point of View* (originally published by Story Press, 2001).

Alexandria's Amazon Author Central Page
Amazon.com/author/alexandriaszeman

Alexandria's Web-Site
AlexandriaConstantinovaSzeman.com

Read excerpts from all her books:
AlexandriaConstantinovaSzeman.com/Books.php

Alexandria's Blog: The Alexandria Papers
TheAlexandriaPapers.com
AlexandriaConstantinovaSzeman.com/Blog.php

Alexandria's Twitter @Alexandria_SZ
Twitter.com/Alexandria_SZ
AlexandriaConstantinovaSzeman.com/Twitter.html

Contact Alexandria
AlexandriaConstantinovaSzeman.com/Contact.php